A Penchant for Masquerades

A Penchant for Masquerades

Poems by Carolyn Martin

Published by Unsolicited Press
www.unsolicitedpress.com

Copyright © 2019 Carolyn Martin
All Rights Reserved.
First Edition Paperback.

Cover Art: Shawn Aveningo Sanders
Book Designer: Nathan Miller
Editor: Kristen Gustafson
Editor: S.R. Stewart

No part of this book may be reproduced or transmitted in any form or by any means without written permission from the publisher or author.

For information, contact the publisher at info@unsolicitedpress.com.

Unsolicited Press Books are distributed to the trade by Ingram.
Printed in the United States of America.
ISBN: 978-1-947021-71-6

For those who have a penchant for doubting
everything and nothing

Contents

Prologue	12
Re-Entry Interview	15
Thoughts on a Translation	17
Searching for Still Life	19
So Are the Days of Our Lives	21
Understudy	22
Phonaesthetics	24
Evidence	26
To the Police Officer Who Let Me Off the Hook	28
For Bob, an Express Parking Lot Bus Driver on the Early Morning Shift at Portland International	30
Attention: Costco General Manager/Re: Why I Returned My Dead Christmas Tree on January 5	32
History	33
"Neanderthals Were People, Too"	35
Here, a Holding On	38
Spoiler Alerts	40
Creative Writing 101: Today's Prompt	42
Four-and-Twenty: A Montage of Disconnected Images	44
What's in a Name?	46
Abishag Finds Her Voice	48
What's Wrong with This Picture? or A Sonnet on Pertinent Questions	50
For God's sake hold your tongue and let me love	51
Sonnet for a 25th Wedding Anniversary	52
Everything Good Between Us	53
Pantoum Conversation	55

10 Variations on the 50 Most Quoted Lines of Poetry	56
Reading *Bailing the River* While Waiting for the Red-Throated Hummingbird to Dine on Crocosmia	59
A Novice's Weekly Confession 1964	61
To Each Her Saint	63
In Dreams Begin Dreams	64
In the Women's Locker Room	65
Almost an Elegy	67
Triolet	69
33 Sententious Epigraphs That May – or Not – Prompt a Poem	70
A Few Words About Inspiration	74
Stirring	76
What I Know of "Good"	78
Haiku: Perennial Wisdom	80
Overheard	82
90+ Titles Appropriated from *Poetry 180* Hosted by Billy Collins	83
Hiking, Formerly Known as Hill Walking	86
Confessions of a Perennial Gardener	87
Not a Pastoral in Five Parts	88
Since feeling comes first . . .	92
Pantoum for the Fallen	93
The Letter I Would Have Written to Wislawa Szymborska Were She Still Alive	94
An Amateur Photographer Reads Szymborska's "No Title Required"	97
Twenty-Five Years After Sodom and Gomorrah: Lot's Older Daughter Makes Her Case	99

Notes from a Water Drinker	101
Requiem for the Dinner Party	103
Disambiguation	105
Caged	107
Variations on Famous Last Words	108
To the Book Reviewer Who Missed Too Much	111
We did all we could	113
Melt Down	115
Saving	118
Should You Ever Start to Pray –	120
A Case for Choosing Sudden Death	121
Epilogue	123

Truth is for tailors and shoemakers. . . .
I, on the contrary, have always held that
the Lord has a penchant for masquerades.
– Isak Dinesen

Prologue

Glasses, hair dye, make-up, pretend expertise, biting wit: fine-tuned strategies to keep others out, me in.

*

Is it more sensible to hem or cobble with the pride of exactitude than to speculate relentlessly on what we cannot understand?

*

Someone said, *Those who chase beasts become beasts*. I say, *Chase Beauty instead*.

*

Set Beauty aside and contemplate the many lies within one Truth, Truths with one lie: Eden and the snake, gods who care, prayers heard – or not, the soundness of a holographic universe, History that repeats, words that mean what they say, life beyond and back again. Although . . . why waste time when garbage must go out, perennials need a plant, and your partner wants a listening?

*

We create our world where there is no shortage of desires or preferences. Every moment something new is born. How does God keep up? Is He/She/It interested?

*

Tending toward heresy, I have a penchant for the man behind Lordly myths. Strip off centuries of masks and there's a wordsmith washing off dust as his wife lays out bread and wine. His mother and siblings with their kids arrive to bless a Sabbath eve. How divine!

*

Believe what you want. I believe failures set us free and eternity holds enough time to get things right.

*

When your face does not add up and your name seems detached, you are a mystery to yourself. Doubt nothing and everything.

*

I've somersaulted and smashed shell-shocked into Newton's "great ocean of truth" where every wave deposits newly broken shards.

*

It's not the fear of cosmic solitude that tosses covers off at three a.m. It's another landscape groaning as it disappears.

*

I couldn't kill the solo ant on my computer screen. She was reading – attentively – the *Poem of the Day*.

*

A theater is *a seeing place*. Lounge in the orchestra, pull out glasses in the mezzanine, squint from the cheap seats. No matter where you sit, Truth struts its poor player self across the stage, signifying something you need signified.

*

Perhaps the actors in your head deserve a better listening.

*

Some authors claim they write to find themselves. Which self? I'd like to know. Mine won't stay still long enough to find a period.

*

What relief to shed this life's go-around. Yet, I will miss my green myopic eyes.

*

When the doctor shoves exhaustion through the OR door – her face set in neutral, gloves and hours slipping off her hands – you know the truth. Yet all you want – before *We did all we could* parts her lips – all you want is one emergent lie, one last second of unshattered peace before no-turning-back. The last thing you want is the ceremony of unrelenting truth.

Re-Entry Interview

Say what? You can't renege now.
We gave you a century of beaches, forests,
and day-trips around the Milky Way.

We re-filled your request for a fine-tuned set
of vocal chords with added tips on how
to project your voice beyond the orchestra.
If you practice hard enough this time,
you might earn a slot on some "Got Talent" show.
Although, as we reminded you before,
success requires discipline and abstinence
from dairy, sugar, and alcohol.

You were right: you were too flabby
your last life so we designed traffic-stopping
breasts and hips with a penchant for styles
you'll adore . . . The catch? Decades of guessing
if you're wanted for your body or your mind.
We guarantee relief when gravity kicks in.
Prepare for the inevitable by working
through *The History of Thought* and buffing up
your magnetic personality.

No, we cannot assure a Pulitzer.
It's up to you to write worthy poetry.
However, we advise against an MFA.
Such academic drudge is unbearable

and the cost makes us choke. Rather,
study Williams, Frost, Yeats, Collins,
Szymborska, Ryan, and Trethewey.
They'll rev you up to roll out of bed,
put the coffee on, and scavenge the day
for what may evolve into a poem.

Come now! It's too late to re-script
you as a pro athlete. That's incongruous
with your new body type and the years
you'll spend learning scales and rhymes.
File this new request as soon as you die
and, if there are roster openings,
we'll set you up with tryouts
for the sport of your choice.

To be blunt, enough is enough.
You've had a refreshing R&R.
Your passport is stamped for next week.

Thoughts on a Translation

Now listen, you watermelons –
if any thieves come,
turn into frogs.
– Issa

*

Issa taught his melons
the art of masquerade
and applauded warty carnivores
chasing poachers away.

*

Would you rather be a watermelon
with its pink flesh cannibalized
or a frog splaying buttered legs
on a gold-trimmed plate?

*

A poet translates Issa's name:
a single bubble in steeping tea.
I prefer *a single frog in a melon patch.*

*

All I know of Issa: a few haiku and Googled facts.
Of watermelons: the etiquette of a silver spoon
scooping fruit, holding slipped-out pits.
Of frogs: quarter-sizes croak above nighthawks,
Beelzebufos ate hatchling dinosaurs.

*

It's discomforting to think
I could slip off this lifetime's
watery pink for a green body
that listens with its mouth.

*

As kids, we learned to love neighbors
who looked like ourselves. How boring:
fields where melons look alike
and frogs sing the same refrain.

*

There is no shortage of imaginary frogs
in real gardens or of bubbles in steeping tea.

*

In the redundancy of dawn, frogs sleep.
Poetry glides through fields,
poaching the silence of watermelons.

*

An ancient painter warned a shoemaker
to stick to his soles and not pretend
expertise about things he does not know.
Not prone to take advice, I'll cobble
a poem about an inept thief who dreams
of stealing melons from a frog-filled pond.

Searching for Still Life

What the old masters learned:
peacocks, bottles, bread, fish, violins,
wine, lobster, crab, vases, candlesticks,
shoemakers' stalls, and barbershops
are more than third-rate art.

Upcycling the vulgar and the vain,
the seasons and the sensual, they laughed
in critics' eyes when canvases flew
from studios to the walls of the rich.
So much for highbrow aesthetics.

★★★

If I could still my life,
      I'd weave bleeding hearts
            through lilac trees,
    camellias into an azalea bush,
and wait until sunrise sneaks through
      fence slats. Snap a photograph.

I'd arrange intimacies –
      face creams, lipsticks, liners, blush –
         in the cabinet above
    the bathroom sink – asymmetrically.
Add a hairbrush, gel, spray, paste,
      an Oral B. Focus the inanimate.

I'd compose lines,
        half-lines down a page. Allude
                to Egypt, France, and the Netherlands.
        Pay homage to Brueghel's bouquet,
Cezanne's cherub, Monet's grapes.
        Bow to synthetics and 3D.

                      ***

Stare long enough and petals brown.
Light dims from pears and mandolins.
Paint peels, reveals the history of dust and awe.
Throw the quantum in and unstillness spins
through spaces between the stars,
between fifteen sunflowers in a vase,
between coins forgotten on a desk.
Does anything remain inanimate?

So Are the Days of Our Lives

If,
for every grain of sand,
ten thousand stars fiddle foot
around the universe,
consider
an hourglass sifting
trillions of galaxies
through indefinite eternity.

That is,
unless Fate forgets a flip.

Then,
futures dissolve,
pasts freeze,
presents grieve
in narrow-necked nothingness.

The sand clock
in *Still Life with a Skull*
begins to peel
and gleeful Death races
to raise
another monument
in the nearest necropolis.

Understudy

To be great one must seem so, and seeming that goes on for a lifetime is no different from reality.
– William Butler Yeats

Friday night.
Blackout shades down, three-way lamp on,
and the woman playing you all day
hangs up her navy suit and white silk blouse.
One high heel hides beneath the bed,
the other stands upright among piles
of books lazing on the hardwood floor.

All week
she strutted into meetings
with practiced words masking uncertainty.
You felt her hold her breath
when hands raised to question or confront.
You felt her exhale
when improv answers arrived on cue.

For years
she's tamped down your blue-collar shame,
raised the ante on style,
quelled blushes and stammering.
She knew you slouched in the mezzanine
while she stole the stage and bowed
to your applauding gratitude.

By ten o'clock,
you've reviewed today's scenes,
noted revisions for next week –
a softer face and tone, a stronger argument.
You're almost convinced she's more you
than you. *Seeming? Reality?*
you quiz the empty room.

Phonaesthetics

*The study of the euphony and cacophony of words
without regard for semantics.*

I read somewhere
that language experts claim
when sense is pushed aside,
the most ear-pleasing English sounds
slide through the words *cellar door.*

Not through the charm
of *velvet/epiphany/
lithe/purple/serendipity/
cinnamon/soliloquy,*
but through the scraped-up entry
to the stale dark space
where my mother scrubbed our clothes
and I escaped upstairs storms.

Cellar door, celadore, seladore –
chant these words out loud
and I'm strolling on Assisi cobblestones
while Cimabue's frescoes peel.
Or flying to the Vegas strip
where gondoliers row arias
beneath a painted sky.
Or settling down in Vinnie's Bar
with friends and pizza pie.

So much for sense
when sounds annihilate cinder blocks,
concrete floors, dank memories.
Three notes – smooth and pure –
soar like kisses from my fingertips
toward the cobbled sky.
Cellar door. Ché bella, cellar door.

Evidence

The fact is I could eat the same meal every day.
The fact is I do.
The fact is I despise playing games.
The fact is I love playing games I can win.
The fact is Druids knocked on wood to startle trees awake.
The fact is I don't like trees observing me.
The fact is behind my façade there's a scared kid who hopes no one calls her out.
The fact is I hate parties unless I'm in charge.
The fact is the hardest character to impersonate is me.
The fact is I prefer the stark mystery of koans to biblical poetry.
The fact is people don't improve much; however, there are exceptions.
The fact is I walk pigeon-toed. Pigeons do it better.
The fact is elbows can't be licked.
The fact is vertical swirls of wine on the glass's side are *legs*.
The fact is arteries pulse different tones in the body's bloody symphony.
The fact is we will be remembered not for what we build, but for what we destroy.
The fact is yetis are more probable than fairies.
The fact is I could be too good to be true, but I am not.
The fact is bunk is bunk and there's lots to go around.
The fact is death is impermanent. Ask any perennial.
The fact is 300-pound gorillas in any room are overrated primates.
The fact is I don't own pets because I fall in love too hard, too fast.
The fact is beauty's felt before it's seen.
The fact is when I can't climb a mountain, it bends its top

toward me.

The fact is when little is at stake, risk is a breeze.

The fact is on this day something happened somewhere.

The fact is happenstance delights more than plans.

The fact is I've filed 97 "Words of the Day" and haven't sentenced one.

The fact is *fact* found print in the 15th century, arriving with *brainless, foolishness, hodgepodge,* and *mockery.*

To the Police Officer Who Let Me Off the Hook

You were right:
eleven miles over sixty-five.
Can't argue with a radar gun.
Fair and clean, you nabbed my Honda Fit
from all those slashing speeders
on the Sunset Highway's curves.

I can tell you now
I almost cited Kepler's Second Law:
planets move faster when
they're nearer to the sun.
I could have teased I was merely
mimicking scientific fact.

I could have spouted lines
written while I drive –
Ten geese hitchhiked
along a puddled road.
I honk, therefore I am.
You honk and you're a jerk –
but I figured fast you wouldn't be amused.

Remember when you said,
Your driver's license, ma'am,
and groaned at,
It's on the kitchen sink?
Remember how you huffed

back to your car to check
my VIN and tally up the fines?

See, here's the truth:
I've raced before. Turned
wrong on one-way streets.
Double-parked. Stole minutes
from the handicapped.
Slipped through dozens of red lights.
You were my only catch
in fifty driving years.

Maybe your quota was full?
Or you recalled last night
dancing your giggling son
around the living room,
watching your daughter's bat zing
in the winning run?
Maybe the heat of making
love softened you?

Whatever the reason,
I need to understand
the terse *Slow down!*
when you returned.
No ticket. No growl.
Nothing beyond two syllables.
Please contact me soon.

For Bob, an Express Parking Lot Bus Driver on the Early Morning Shift at Portland International

His breathy *hello*
and corny jokes
endear
even when we're half-awake,
grieving warm bodies
left behind,
wary of the stress ahead.
(Snow, forecasts claim,
threatens O'Hare.
Expect delays.)

Did you hear the one about . . .?
What happens when . . .?
Non-stop diversions
earn our groans.
He pockets them
like lost coins
and enjoys a quip
thrown back.

Every stop
his parental voice:
This is station (number)
in the (color) zone.
If you got on here,
write it down.

At the terminal,
Share a smile today,
and off he drives
to seat
another audience.

A week gone.
After lonely hotel
rooms and
mediocre food,
cell phones
on the return bus
report
to whoever needs
to hear:
On the ground.
Love you. Soon.

It's night.
No Bob. No jokes.
My mind, a blank.
But here,
scribbled across
a sales receipt:
blue zone, station three.

Attention: Costco General Manager/ Re: Why I Returned My Dead Christmas Tree on January 5

Knock on wood, they say,
but three weeks of watering your Douglas fir
and all I got were needles messing up
my rugs, sticking to my shoes.

Did you see the debris
around your *Returns* door?
You might want to sweep it up before
someone slides and sues for more
than Bailey's, Bayer's, and Ben Gay.

This return has nothing to do
with *self-respect* or *dignity*
like that snobby guy behind me swore.
I own both but here are facts you need to chew:
K-Mart poinsettias are still in half-bloom.
Safeway sugar cookies, semi-fresh.
Sears re-stocked my once-worn-only Christmas dress.

Count on this: next year I'll find a farm
that grows Noble firs. (They're guaranteed
to last beyond Epiphany.) I'll decorate
and take a photograph in the new year.
Expect a 4x6 in a recycled card.

History

(with a nod to Kay Ryan)

In the thick of it,
who knows
when or if
they're
making it.
Take scientists
who shovel
facts.
For decades,
they agreed
Lucy led
the pack.
Then,
they modernized
the story line
when Little Foot –
fully formed –
reset the pace.
With History
on their backs,
sifters keep
sifting through
time and space.
So much for
certainty

when
bone-bound Truth
hides out
in sediment
for centuries.

"Neanderthals Were People, Too"

– Jon Mooallem, *New York Times*, January 11, 2017

1. *In a valley not yet named Neander, 40,000 BC*

It wasn't the size of our brains –
we could match them wit for wit –
or climate change or epidemics.

It wasn't a resource grab
or being clubbed to death
by human supremacists.

Numbers doomed us in the end.
We were swamped. They trickled
in dribs and drabs in tiny bands –

a species almost on par.
We could have hung around
another thousand years except

for a fact history won't bear:
we chose to disengage.
We could see it in those eyes tucked

beneath slanting brows: they'd wipe
each other out before earth collapsed –
created, as they were, to be themselves.

Nothing random about our drift.
Intuition, not luck. We elected to die
rather than devolve to live like them.

2. *From Homo sapiens, USA, 2019*

In the beginning, we
        bungled it.
Without precise
        technology,
we improvised our ignorance:

They walked on all fours.
        Never laughed.
Wallowed in morass.
        Losers at best.
Ogres at worst.

Measured by prospects
        so low, their name
bandied about
        derisively.
Yet . . . what intelligence

in shapers of flint
        and fine toothpicks,
featherers of hair,
        mixers of high-heat glue
that still stumps scientists.

They spoke in voices,
        raspy and high-pitched,
built bedrooms in caves,
        bred and interbred
without prejudice.

Today, geneticists claim
        we maintain 1–2%
of their DNA.
        If only there
were more. If only . . .

Here, a Holding On

For New York City

October 1, 2001

Twenty days of barricades
and twos and threes pause
on Chambers Street –
business suits, backpacks, hoodies,
police uniforms in every size.
No one pontificates
over vacant desks and pews,
tear-wet beds, fire stations gone,
bone fragments searching for home.

Here, they're awed.
Tower shadows fled.
The first time in thirty years
Village streets and living rooms,
store fronts with their sidewalk signs,
responders struggling with ash
bathe in sun. They bathe in the sun.

I, a stranger from 3,000 miles west,
grab a subway strap,
head to an uptown hotel
to write this down.

August 7, 2017

Here, breaking news:
DNA defines one more loss.
(Male. Unnamed. Per family request.)

Who's left?

Eleven hundred twelve gathered
in dusty dark, sharing thoughts
they thought as shadows dissolved.
Comparing notes on deals signed,
dinners served, dreams deferred
for the practicalities of work,
little words unsaid.

Here, holding on –
each to each –
until they're freed from this room
where they've agreed
on the coarsest truth:
closure is a myth.

Spoiler Alerts

In this prequel to *East of Eden*, an unrepentant Adam and Eve admit they ate the snake not the apple.

*

After Humpty-Dumpty falls to pieces, all the King's horses and all the King's men celebrate over fish, chips, and micro-brew in a London pub.

*

Three not-so-little pigs are condemned to the weight-list for barbeque.

*

Sunday's Child, masquerading as *bonny and blithe and good and gay,* is outed as a melancholic hetero.

*

Old Mother Hubbard and Little Boy Blue are covers for a cross-dressing Cardinal.

*

Hey, Diddle, Diddle: Disney fiddles with a cat and sends a cow over the moon. The little dog shouts, *Hey, nonny, no, sports!* as the dish out-dashes the spoon.

*

In this sequel to *Water Pail Hill*, Jack and Jill (aka Louis XVI and Marie Antoinette) lose their heads. Severed crowns held up high scan the masses with baleful eyes. You may want to avert yours.

*

A year after the royal wedding, Cinderella hurls unwearable shoes into the scullery hearth.

*

In 2035, two grain-fed chickens cross the road to nothing on the other side.

*

After centuries of material experiments, the London Bridge collapses during a holographic glitch.

*

Reincarnating humanoids decide to check out before they check in. They opt for miscarriages rather than toxic air.

*

After myriads of miscues, God concedes the male seahorse that births its young and the leafy dragon fish floating in wedding white are among the few that evolved perfectly.

Creative Writing 101: Today's Prompt

Think of a time
when freeways
wore miles of mud
and oceans covered
mountain tops;
the time before
human prints
unequalized
playing fields
and animals
commandeered forests
and flower beds.

Create columns
labeled
nouns, verbs,
descriptive words.
Clarify differences.
Circle favorites.

Eliminate
complexity.
Simple sounds
will hold
their strength.
Birth them
into lines

or paragraphs.
Focus on
vitality.

Research epigraphs
like *In the beginning, God.*
or *A journey's not complete
until its story's told.*

Do not confuse
truth with facts,
facts with myths.

Four-and-Twenty: A Montage of Disconnected Images

Panhandlers scrounge on ramps.
Will work for food and gas.
You veer a lane away.
Shame, their toothless faces scowl.

⁕

An African violet squats – self-watered
and content – before a coffee mug,
bowl, and poems hungering
for help. Sip. Spoon. Revise.

⁕

Beige: boring, neutral, nondescript.
But wait: the color of tightly wound
magnolia buds contains
a fuzzy fallow before spring arrives.

⁕

Yesterday we woke in the right house
in the wrong room.
Today the room turned right.
The house has fled.

⁕

The air breathes hot at 8 a.m.
Mourning doves struggle

to catch their songs.
It's too dense to remember dreams.

*

While Baja humpbacks teach
their calves to breach and expats tee
off on Pamilla's green,
we wallow in winter snow.

*

You have the right to remain
silent, but judgment flashes
through your green eyes
and how you cross your legs.

What's in a Name?

Day lilies come
and go by the clock.
Evergreens remain.
The devil frog
horrifies.
And there's
the Milky Way,
the whitish smudge
that, like a toddler
burping up,
spews messy gas
across the universe.

Which leads me to
our micro-galaxy.
In the blur
of everyday,
we're lover/
partner/
friend
with an appetite
for constancy
that soaks in
tiffs and blame,
rings out kisses
and regrets.

But what if
we recalibrate?
Let's call ourselves
excited atoms
on an errant star
shooting through
a dozen Milky Ways –
not caring
where we are –
like reckless
first-borns in
a pre-name paradise.
Or something
close to that.

Abishag Finds Her Voice

(1 *Kings* 1–4)

More blankets. Now!
I shouted to his gawking men,
and fuel that fire to a rage.

Whoever thought virginity would thaw
a dying King thought wrong.
No matter how rigorous my thighs,

how tight my arms around his wrinkled skin,
youth can't do the trick. Days and nights,
Where are his eighteen wives? I ask –

those who felt his heat, who knew the hands
that rocked a giant down. Where are they now?
Afraid he wouldn't know their names? Wouldn't care?

Wise ones say I have a mind of my own
and the comeliness of Eve. They will place me
among the worthy women of the world.

But here behind closed doors, trying
to revive their hero/murderer/king,
I am attendant/nurse/whore.

Tonight: *Make me a queen or set me free.*
My fiery words blush his fading face.

I hold my ground. Insist. He turns away.

Here's to good death. I throw lambswool
over his shaking limbs. *Who would be proud
to claim a house that bears your name?*

Cursing the crackling fire, I brush
his grieving lords aside. *Think on that,*
I whisper to the freezing walls. *Think on that.*

What's Wrong with This Picture? or A Sonnet on Pertinent Questions

Are you kidding me? Friends jump off a cliff
and I was raised by wolves? A truth or dare?
Big Bang or God? A Spanish pope? What if
the hen crossed back again? Knock. Knock. Who's there?
What happened to that twinkling little star?
What do you expect? Who's the boss? The man?
To be or not? How much? How long? How far?
Where have all the flowers gone? Understand,
if I compared you to a summer's day,
you'd ask for tell-and-show. So what about
a poem on how you're loved a thousand ways?
The answers may surprise, and they'll point out –
beyond a truthful dare – that wolves are shy
and skies are more than blue, so why ask why?

For God's sake hold your tongue and let me love

the avalanche of maple leaves landing
on the grass as autumn thunder claps

sun shooting through fence holes
like lighthouse lamps that lost their wink

the feral sitting in the jasmine pot
laughing at stellar jays stalking squirrels

the emails you send on "How Not to Die"
mine on pruning myrtle and japonica

the right to remain silent you ignore
when you instruct me to listen fast

the way you hug curves, I the centerline
how you're perennial, I'm annual

why you're the music on my stand
the architect at my drawing board

how we're immune to recriminate
how we're diagnosed for happiness

Sonnet for a 25th Wedding Anniversary

She came to me in the rain.
– James Wright, "Sappho"

What a silly thing to do, this Memory
without umbrella or boots, slipping through
the drenching afternoon, reminding me
of all the loves I filed away. A few
headlined *puppy-ish* with clipped good-byes,
bewilderment, words enraged, slamming doors.
One *six-month-stand* that could not survive
my fear of settling in, succeeded by four
*if-only*s and two *might-have-beens*. And now,
from miles of time away, I bless each prelude
to today. Relieved, I stroll through rows
of dripping irises with gratitude
to all my left-behinds. Memory sighs,
See. Nothing is recalled the same way twice.

Everything Good Between Us

I have no ear for singing and seldom land on a black or white. *Listen in your head*, you say when I change keys five times. *I'm scatting*, I try. *Good luck with that*, your reply.

Whoever is in the driver's seat is incompetent. My gas pedal foot never behaves and my mind strays off the road. *You're writing poems again*, you call me back. *Where are we going?* I ask.

You strut your Nordstrom's strut through the mall, dismissing a dozen clothing stores by the time I consider one. Quintessence of style, you lament my disregard for what I wear.

Everything defaults to me: the glasses you lost somewhere, the key that doesn't fit, the celery I bought that wasn't plump enough. Trade-off? You ignore my grumpiness.

You have to listen faster, you complain when I ask for a repeat. I can't keep up when you allegro through health, finance, politics, and theology.

The time between a rift and a reconcile grows shorter every year. We slam doors, conjure up a laugh, reconnect to our own happiness. And, ah! there's always that kiss.

In every grocery store, I turn right, you turn left. I'm the counter-, you're the -wise. Inevitably, at noon or midnight we meet – you with salty, me with sweet.

When I invite you to talk about death, you reply, *I haven't tried it yet.* When I say, *Then talk about miracles*, you smile, *What's the difference?*

When chaos sneaks up and threatens our equanimity, we look it in the eye, grab each other's hands, and dance to the music of the spheres.

When I run out of things to write, I'll pose you against a baby grand like Barbra, Liza, or Elaine belting out show tunes to the neighborhood. Everything about you sings a poem.

Pantoum Conversation

Contentment is the death of bliss,
I said – or was it you who said? –
I with my dry wit, you with your long-sightedness.
Let's talk about death,

I said – or was it you who said? –
Old age is a bitch that won't last long.
Let's talk about death.
Not interested, you said.

Old age is a bitch that won't last long.
Let's grieve the loss of bliss, you said.
Not interested, I said
and offered you a passing kiss.

Let's grieve the loss of bliss, you said.
To each her saint, I said
and offered you a passing kiss:
a warm ember on a flameless fire.

To each her saint, I said –
I with my dry wit, you with your long-sightedness.
A warm ember on a flameless fire,
contentment is not bliss.

10 Variations on the 50 Most Quoted Lines of Poetry

1.
If music be the food of love,
Candy / Is dandy / But liquor / Is quicker.

2.
The proper study of mankind
is my mistress' eyes –
a joy forever.

3.
I think that I shall never see.

4.
To be or not to be
a rose – a dangerous thing:
truth . . . beauty . . . all.

5.
Do not go gentle,
O, Romeo,
in Flanders fields where poppies blow.
Humankind cannot bear
to err.

6.
Things fall apart.
Stop the clocks, cut off the telephone.
The time has come,
but at my back I always hear
'tis better to have loved,
to only stand and wait,
not to yield.

7.
Lend me your ears,
band of brothers.
The father of the man
full fathom five . . . lies
in Xanadu with fortune
and men's eyes.

8.
If you can keep your head,
busy old fool,
tread softly
like a narrow fellow in the grass.

9.
Because I could not stop for death,
I am the master of my fate.
Look on my works –
the moving finger writes
seasons of mist and the old lie.
We have no time to stand and stare.

The mind is its own place
where hope springs eternal.

10.
Let me count the ways
I grow old lonely as a cloud.
I shall wear purple
and talk of many things –
the quality of mercy,
a summer's day,
a bang . . . a whimper;
protest too much the miles
to go before I sleep.

Reading *Bailing the River* While Waiting for the Red-Throated Hummingbird to Dine on Crocosmia

– For Penelope Scambly Schott
in honor of Lily, the White Dog

By the time I get to page 79
where your book's title first appears –
tucked between buckets and mops
and a bathtub drain; between young belief
death isn't real and the world can be saved –
coyotes are sniffing sadness.

They know it's true: there is no grief
more reliable than for a white dog who used
up her world and left dinner plates
unrinsed in a kitchen sink.

Maybe she's gone to find a lost uncle
to confirm his smell. Perhaps to track the doe
she chased over the barbed wire fence.
(Her heart wants forgiveness.)
She might be frisking in the forest
where trees caper ecstatically
or beside Frost's horse stopping on a snow-soft night.
She might be listening to Emily think through
why she could not stop for death. Why not?
The mind wants to imagine these things.

How life wants to go on living, you write
on page 82, so there's no consolation yet.
Someday birds will mute their screams
and you'll tell Lily stories until they bail out
your tears. You won't fail to include
she honored poet friends by not barking
while they read and claimed a title in her name.
You'll be sure to add how she snubbed
your husband's offer for a walk
whenever you were home
and how she knew we're passengers
on a frisky planet we don't own.
Dogs are wise that way.

In case you're curious,
by the time I closed your book,
the hummingbird had not arrived.
The Crocosmia and I will wait and imagine
a white dog prancing across the yard.

A Novice's Weekly Confession
1964

Noonday prayer and the conjuring of venial flaws:
eyes raised too high, coffee spills, a veil scorched
by an iron set too hot. You'll save whispering
after Sacred Silence rings and overdosing
on ice cream to supplement next week.

You ease your faults through the grille
to the priest who listens and cajoles.
He jokes about ironing boards and coffee pots,
instructs on accidents.
A penance worthy of crimes?
Three Hail Marys and an hour's walk outside.

Prayers dashed off, you grab your shawl.
Unforeseen: in twenty years
fine-lined eyes, brows, and lips
above a business suit commanding
crowds with authority and grace.
Unpredictable: each hotel night –
room service cleared, sheets turned down –
a habit and veil wear you in your dreams.

But today you are nineteen – a lover
of sunrise chants, chores, studies, rosaries –
set on holiness, awake in black and white.
The tower clock strikes one and wool shields

nipping winds. Eyes rising toward
chartreuse leaves, you smile at their unraveling.

To Each Her Saint

Canonize? The prize
for two miracles.
Not much to ask,
considering.
Someone walks upright,
banishes unruly cells,
faces off
the voices in her head,
stops a river's rise:
triumphs claimed
in an almost-saint's name.

For those of us
who dismiss titles
and candles lit
on flowered altars
in a namesake church,
we elect
to venerate a dad
stacking barrels
of paint for years
on the merciless concrete
of a factory floor.

Dreams Begin Dreams

Look – down the sidewalk's weed-cracked curves, your chubby teenage self holds hands with a wrinkled aunt who spits obscenities across the neighbor's lawn. You duck behind an incense fir to strip your jeans and don a nun-black dress for a moment that lasts twenty years. Time stretches your soul before you sashay blue suits into conference rooms to teach empty chairs the latest business tips. Your disheveled script hides in a roller bag that drags you across burnt sand to Maui's edge where turtles line coral reefs to hear you rant in free verse. Snorkel-geared, you dive toward white beds and strip to zaftig flesh. No lover's touch down there, so you rise through the sun-rayed waves, tender kisses to yourself, and wake your body in your own embrace.

In the Women's Locker Room

Without a thought, we slough off bathing suits and caps
and kick them away from the shower's heat.
Nothing's left between soap and aprons of fat,
thinning head and pubic hair, exhausted breasts.

We know each other well
and the husband who can't find his way back home,
the son who failed at suicide-by-cop,
the boss who made us kneel.

This morning we debate *Golden Girls* reruns:
from Dorothy's designer clothes
to what gets more laughs:
Rose's naiveté or Blanche's sluttiness.
We wish we were Sophia-sharp
with her tart put-downs and *Picture this* . . .

Rather than grousing about the news,
we committed months ago to ritual:
swim, shower, cheer for the camaraderie
that lets us be who we are. No fear
of tears or scars. No holding back.

We haven't grabbed our towels yet
when three high school goddesses prance by.
Bikinied, svelte, and glorious, they freeze –
hands-over-mouths horrified –

and can barely bare to look.

We wave them smiles and somehow know –
perhaps from decades of growing wise –
no matter how fast or far they flee,
nothing – not prom dates, scholarships,
or first-place trophies – will erase this scene.
We dry off. They run the other way.

Almost an Elegy

Just between you and me, I don't know where
my head's been. My days are so mixed up,
I forgot all about this afternoon's cake and tea.
I'll put the kettle on. You grab the cups
and flowered plates and we'll cozy down.

Stop me if you heard this before – I hate it
when people can't keep their listeners straight –
anyway, it used to be I could tally
groceries in my mind faster than cashiers
could tap them in. I'd breeze through diagramming
sentences the nun chalked on the board,
and the Catechism answers she claimed were true?
I'd bounce them back at her word for word for word.

But now most days my brain absconds –
I've lost the bills I readied for the mail.
Can't recall if daffodils arrive
before or after candytufts.
As for why God created us? Long gone.

Be careful, the cup is hot. And, look,
the glazing has melted down the cake like
icicles announcing winter's passing on.
My, that almost sounds like poetry! Anyway . . .
there's something important you must know:
my neighbors say they share my malady.

The fact is I've got it worse. Most times
I forget their names and mine slips out the door.
Truth be told, today I almost misplaced yours.

Before you go . . . Don't be silly.
That's not a hint. I love your company . . .
Before you go, I need you to tell me
what to do. No soft-pedaling around
with a *maybe* or *perhaps*. Please wipe
that pity off your face and tell me what
to do. Someday I may stroll out too far
and not come back. Every day it's harder
to know if the sun's rising up or slipping down.
Tell me. I'm not sure of anything.

Triolet

I can't recall the season – this,
last, to come. They blur into one
soft shape where edges don't exist.
I can't recall the season. This
one: leaves on snow on crocuses;
last: icy roses bloom. Undone,
I can't recall the season – this,
last, to come. They blur into one.

33 Sententious Epigraphs That May – or Not – Prompt a Poem

The purpose of writing poems is to save epigraphs.
– Kay Ryan

In the beginning, God.

*

What's a twist of facts when truth rings true?

*

The letters spelling *death* are not death.

*

Contentment is the death of bliss.

*

What's useful to know when nothing's just itself?

*

A journey's not complete until its story's told.

*

Give me a mask and I will show you who I am.

*

Randomness: an order we've yet to understand.

*

I think it's true and I don't like it: Laws make criminals of us all.

*

You can be forgiven for thinking nothing – or thinking that nothing is as perfect as *what-might-have-been*.

*

Choices navigate what is. Memories re-navigate what was.

*

Stop interrupting me while I'm interrupting someone else.

*

Be yourself unless you can be a gosling, then be a gosling.

*

There's more to you than you.

*

We almost had it all and then we realized we didn't want it all.

*

Love is a brush with promises.

*

The navel I've been gazing on is yours.

*

The fly in a spider's web, the spider in a wasp's death-grasp, the wasp in a honey buzzard's beak: Karma's seamlessness.

★

When a solo ant climbs two floors to rest on your toilet seat, how can you fear solitude?

★

The ease of the gift does not take away from the gratitude.

★

The Big Bang created time: the prison we're bound in.

★

There's no direction in space. Getting lost is simple in every way.

★

Rubberneckers slow down to assure themselves the body lying in the road is not theirs.

★

Ignore expiration dates. Leave death to professionals and damn the consequence.

★

Death is the ellipsis between two lives.

★

When the wind's too far to rouse our sails, what's left to guide us home?

*

I'm not listening, but I don't want to appear as if I'm not listening.

*

Does the ash remember wood? Does smoke remember ash? Does the wind know what it carries through the firs?

*

I can't take credit for good soil, wind-borne seeds, or multiplying bulbs; but mine's the strong back and cracked fingernails.

*

Catbird seat: sitting pretty with the upper hand: my kind of resting place.

*

Stop to notice and you're saved.

*

I feel like I'm two feet behind myself

*

Some days God is embarrassed to be God.

A Few Words About Inspiration

It happens this way: the day collects stuff:
a squirrel in rigor on a cottage stone,
chemtrails staining summer's sky,
a white spider on the TV screen.

A toilet flush, furnace fan, cars crunching down
a crumbling road, planes nicking clouds,
sunrise bouncing off the house
lighting daisies in hinoki shade.

Every moment something new appears,
each longing to be raked, piled, flamed
into lines that may, as Frost dictates,
begin their slide toward wisdom from delight.

Wouldn't he love the smallest architect
taking a spinning-break from web design?
Work needs a few deep breaths, he'd say,
and time to hear the neighbor's scythe swish
beyond unmended walls, to smell apples
basketed for market or cider press.

He'd stop at gashes near the squirrel's heart
and confer with a stellar jay.
This death? No accident, they'd claim.
What mischief in a creature that carves
red marks, then skulks away?

What would wisdom say?

The sky cleansing itself,
the spider coaxed out the slider door,
intrusions of sounds and light – up for grabs.
What mystery designed earth to spin
into a perfect prompting place?

Stirring

1.
Juncos stagger through
sun-swirling firs, praise
the revival of day.

2.
The alarm commands,
Out of bed!
Curiosity waits.

3.
Headlines disquiet.
Not even a mouse
expects peace on earth.

4.
Music hops the fence
from the neighbor's yard.
My coffee's hot. Who cares?

5.
Recipes demand *beat,*
mix, blend, fold, whip, whisk.
Soufflés require nuances.

6.
The oiled wok: broccoli,
bok choy, onion, ginger,
carrots collaborate.

7.
Obsession agitates,
ends with a swizzle stick
in frosted glass.

8.
Hullabaloos fire up
compatible compatriots:
-crazy, –able, -up, -about.

9.
Circles motivate
imagination and memory
to a firm consistency.

10.
A sign provokes:
Give me ambiguity
or something else.

What I Know of "Good"

Bad things are going to happen.
– Ellen Bass, "Relax"

Perennials return without a thought
and so do volunteers from maples
and japonica. Nature recruits
another nursery at no extra cost.

Lab tests uncover few deficiencies.
Extra pounds aggravate,
but knees hold up and pressure
sits almost where it ought to be.

The computer has worked with ease
for months and my clamshell –
one hinge broke – still performs
like a phone without accessories.

There's no husband to complain
about or children to invest life in.
A fresh pot of coffee brews
and rain clouds hide the sun.

I'll pop five thousand mgs
of vitamins and prescribe
myself to stay indoors to iron
out complexities

of Samaritans, Fridays, grief,
times, advice, reviews,
movies, books, friends, food –
anything *good* antecedes.

Haiku: Perennial Wisdom

early spring chill
and the universe in my hands
a cup of hot tea

weeks of chartreuse –
young leaves erase
months of winter gray

morning alert –
earthworms, hold your breath
robins on the lawn

a hummingbird dines
on orange Crocosmia
I close my notebook

a far-sighted spider spins
on a "Do Not Enter" sign
hunger strikes

listen up, you frogs –
if poachers sneak in at dawn,
hide your muscled legs

crisped leaves
scud down the street
fall's rain stick

death's a name
for life-at-rest
perennial wisdom

on a winter night
the black echo of my breath
my sole company

through many lifetimes
boil water, make tea, drink
one ceremony

Overheard

As evening sneaks around
the house,
the ironing board and
kitchen sink gossip about
your first kiss.
Inexplicable – how
they understand the intimacy
of wind-brushed clouds; how,
in this chartreuse spring,
you'll leave behind
your baseball glove for moony moods
and un-chewed fingernails; how
you'll charge
summer's quickenings
with shattered
beliefs of black and white.
Tonight, as the board folds itself
and the last dish is washed,
the owl clock hushes
their surmise.
If you had overheard, you
would have entertained
their slivered truths,
perhaps cheered their prophecy.

90+ Titles Appropriated from *Poetry 180* Hosted by Billy Collins

One morning walking home through the meadow –
the green one over there – God said yes
to me and the heat and the blue willow
and the hard shadows and the red wing.
How bright it was: this unconditional day,
this moment, the summer I was sixteen.

*

The courtesy of the blind:
the Cape May Warbler who flew against my window.
She didn't mean to do it.

*

You're so beautiful it's starting to rain:
a love song for my daughter
on a summer day.

*

Advice from the experts:
Change a frog into a prince.
Offer gratitude to old teachers.
Tell your Mother there will be no grandkids in her future.

*

I've been known to help a monkey cross
the river, toast the Baltimore Oriole,

feed the swan at Edgewater Park.
It took all my energy.

*

The poetry of bad weather:
a herd of buffalo crossing the Missouri
on ice, the last wolf, bat, snow: gone.
The dress rehearsal for the end and the beginning.

*

Because you left me a handful of daffodils,
the blue bowl, my father's hats,
the family photo around the Xmas tree,
I listen to immortality.

*

Soccer moms:
morning swim
Tuesday 9:00 a.m.,
coffee in the afternoon,
then the ode to dirt.

*

Ladies and gentlemen in outer space:
after years of distances,
thanks for remembering us
on your forgotten planet.
Notice proof of life.

*

The hymn of a fat woman:
decades of exotic treats,
slumnights in loud music halls,
stammering before she died,
Do you love me?

*

Walking to Oak-Head Pond,
and thinking of the ponds
I will visit in the next days and weeks:
entrance to summer happiness.
What would I do otherwise?

*

Any advice for those of us just starting out?
Question numbers, the death of Santa Claus,
and the partial explanation of the good life.
When death comes, fast break toward clouds
and the small comfort of the moon.

*

Thanks to the poet
who burns for the perfection of paper.

Hiking, Formerly Known as Hill Walking

Tilden Park, California

Walking hills
is leisure.
Poppies spill
through lupine
and your eyes
pleasure
in Shar-pei wrinkles
lying
golden thick.
A coddiwomple
deserving
a walking stick.

But slip off
one syllable
like a heel-holed sock
and the trek
becomes misery:
backpacks, boots,
supplies to stretch
for miles
end with
the blistered boast
you hiked.

Confessions of a Perennial Gardener

Six nurseries ago, I said, *I'm through*.
Colors cozied up in my backyard, five dozen pots
brimmed full, and Nature praised, *More is less.*
Anyway, I had little planting time or space
and proclaimed a midsummer freeze.

That is, until *Perennial sale this week*!
How their names enticed: Elegance Snow
cooling Arctic Fire, Peptalk Pink stirring
with Red Rum, Funfare Yellow hovering
over Pixie Blues. Each multi-life a guarantee
to fill the gap annuals leave behind
and fight against the fret of frost.

The choice? Ignore their tags' advice
and squeeze them into tightnesses
between petunias and marigolds,
behind lines of pansies and mums,
under the semi-shade of maple trees.

More is more: my new rule.
When every bloom has dropped, I'll wrap
my roots around those tucked in last.
We'll breathe in winter's depths,
dream of lives to come,
and celebrate death's impermanence.

Not a Pastoral in Five Parts

These things/Astonish me beyond words.
– William Carlos Williams, "Pastoral"

1.
No rural itch
and what I know of sheep
could fill one line.

I prefer milkmaids
invested in the Dow,
shepherds who own
Victorians in town,
and the local news
bemoaning
the death of malls.

Here's to tasting
vineyards in restaurants
and traipsing through
Fields in Spring
under soft museum lights.

Up with urban sprawl
where chickens lay
eggs in neighborhoods
and herons pluck
koi from designer ponds.

Cheers for bucolic dreams
where buxom lasses
plow across meadows
of traffic lights
for rolls in organic hay.

Who wouldn't rhapsodize
landscapes
idyllically citified?

2.
When you asked
me to take down
the plum tree,
I took you literally.

To the ground,
I heard,
although I loved
its flowering.

You yelled,
A trim! too late.
We bemoan
empty space.

3.
If, when the house is empty
and the kitchen clock

counterpoints the furnace
playing off and on
and the plane droning overhead –

if, when a poem, the one
about time and space,
decides it's done and lopes
off the computer screen
into a file of its own –

if, when the garage door
begins its rise
and your horn invites
me to grab my shoes
to help with groceries –

if, when we unpack
steak, broccoli, chips,
and a day's worth
of stories catching up
with themselves –

if I could be more content,
I can't imagine it.

4.
We're warned:
a frigid sea will crash at dawn.
One day to shut gardens down
before icy snow smothers

dahlias, mums, roses, and bamboo.

I've mudded through
autumn rains, mis-heeding
weather prophecies.
Thorns slash my glove-free hands
and freezing dirt clogs
my moonless nails.

Despite the cold,
I cut and rake urgency.
Daylight's winding down.
There's no reprieve
from spiteful seas.
We're warned:
the world is shutting down.

5.
It goes with saying – the way
a willow's waves say wind,
rains say bounty or flood,
fires say death and rebirth –
this must be said: Earth
is uncertain it will endure.

Since feeling comes first...

– e.e. cummings

       . . . why bother with thought?
Ask any riled wave or wind-swept gull.
They do what they do without studying
tidal charts or Bernoulli's principle.

Electric bees in wildflower fields
or mother seals prodding pups to shore?
No conferencing with expert botanists
or sophists on the art of parenting.

Who surrenders to *Love at first thought*?
Even *at first sight* is not exact. Try
pondering: *Love, like Life and Death and all
the in-betweens, feels before it sees or thinks.*

Pantoum for the Fallen

(360 km west of Kathmandu, September 8, 2008)

A natural or supernatural calamity?
Three thousand trees collapse. Five per second.
Ten minutes on the dot. No gales or storms.
No clock. No barometer. No scientific certainty.

Three thousand trees collapse. Five per second.
From centuries of trees shushing one-hand claps?
No clock. No barometer. No scientific certainty.
An omen, locals claim. Of what? All we know

from centuries of trees shushing one-hand claps:
the earth shifts beneath our souls.
An omen, locals claim. Of what? All we know:
roots free themselves to feel the sun

as the earth shifts beneath our souls
and we become groundlessness.
As roots free themselves to feel the sun,
collapses unveil mysteries.

We become groundlessness
in ten minutes on the dot. No gales or storms.
Collapses unveil mysteries.
A natural supernatural calamity?

The Letter I Would Have Written to Wislawa Szymborska Were She Still Alive

Dear Ms. Szymborska,

This is just to say I cannot
delight in your poems enough.
Your subversive subtlety bamboozling
tyranny was worth the Nobel Prize.

How you out-Brueghel-ed
the painter with your *Two Monkeys* dream!
Who else admits they *don't know
what to say* to most everything?

I adored "May 16, 1973," my birthday.
The date didn't ring your bell,
but school bells hustled me to class.
You would have giggled
with my teens when I donned
Shaw's white beard to imitate,
I was a virgin until I was twenty-eight.

I confess "Tortures" was tortuous
to read. *Nothing has changed,*
you don't relent, except *more people
and new offenses* causing grief.

I had to skip to "Slapstick"

where angels – if they exist –
clap their wings and laugh at movies,
comically silent and disastrous.

That's how you pace your poems,
correct? When horror overwhelms,
you opt for playfulness.
What relief, this breathing space!

It's not inconceivable
you and I could be great friends.
We would share babka recipes,
color Easter eggs, smear horseradish
on kielbasa between slices of black bread.
I like to dream these things.

Would you ask your translator
to send the phonetic spelling
of your first name? Here, water
is water, vice is vice. I'm confused
about Polish consonants.

Also, please include your intent
in "Conversation with a Stone."
Friends and I disagree. I assure them
the horse's mouth will breathe the truth,
even if she says she doesn't know.

One more thing before I close:
here's a poem in response

to your "No Title Required."
I chose to title my mine – no offense.

An Amateur Photographer Reads Szymborska's "No Title Required"

This is how the morning starts:
She's sitting under a tree beside a river
having arrived there from somewhere else.
I'm on my patio waiting for August heat
to diminish last night's chill.
She postulates unimportant details ground
the earth. We agree to agree.

Take the sprinklers that did their job at dawn.
The bees committed – whole-bodily –
to last-gasping blooms.
Or the spider dropping from the maple tree
to read my pencil-noted book.

Nothing earth-quaking here,
but who would want to live without?

I admit, if I were under her poplar tree
at the Raba's edge, I'd turn my camera
toward the everyday of riversides.
There: accidents of light, half-bent limbs,
clouds reflecting in swathes of calm.
Here: my eye framing unimportant things,
offering them eternity.

But today is her *insignificant event*

where every detail signifies: the *fertile past*,
wind/ants/grass, coronations and conspiracies.
Each the quiddity of circumstance,
each merging each-with-each.

Here's something I'd want her to understand:
Without a witty thought, I'd wait
for a butterfly to settle on a willow branch.
Without a wise thought, I'd expect its shadow to arrive.
Without any thought at all, I'd bow my camera
toward this trinity, letting river backgrounds blur.
I'd be content with that, I'd want her to know.
Without a fanfare of doubt, I'd be content.

Twenty-Five Years After Sodom and Gomorrah: Lot's Older Daughter Makes Her Case

(This interview has been edited for clarity and length.)

Incest? Call it securing legacy.
When your world is pulverized,
what else would you expect?

Our plan? Two nights plus two daughters
equal two sons to carry our bloodline.
Brothers/sons, sons/grandsons.
How's that for lineage?

On the ridge in a cave.
Oh, what an ugly thing: a soused old man
with lusty dreams that weren't dreams.
At first dawn-light, I remember how he glared,
rubbed his grizzled frown, glared again.
Scared? Confused? Aroused?
We hid our laughter in the waking wind.

Guilty? Of what?
What father offers daughters to a mob?
Our rape for his guests' sodomy?
Call that righteousness? We called it treachery.
Anyway, those strangers in our house?
They weren't men . . . Angels, of course.
If you're up on the literature, they arrive

when their god seems like he cares.
Ask our cousin Isaac. An angel called off
his father's knife, but what god even asks?

Our mother? Now there's a tragedy.
Don't look back. Did she even hear?
When you're wrenched from home,
senses collapse and there's no time
for reasoning out a consequence.
A pillar for an over-shoulder glance?
All she did was send a last good-bye
to friends she didn't criticize.
Where's the wrong in that?

No. I don't know if he ever saw himself
in Moab's eyes or in the way Ammon frowned,
or if he realized what their names meant.
You're interested? "From my father" / "son of my kin."
The truth? I don't think he ever thought to care.

Write this down to set the record straight:
we never walked behind, never looked back.

Notes from a Water Drinker

*No poems can please for long or live
that are written by water drinkers.*
– Horace

Imagine hanging out with a guy who speaks
aphoristically and pontificates over flasks of wine.

He teases about my half-full water cup
and claims my attempts at sober poetry

aren't worth his time. I throw him a dig
when he spouts, *Whatever advice you give, be short,*

reminding him he contradicts himself:
When I struggle to be brief, he's said, *I become obscure.*

Short advice? Vague brevity? There's a poem
in here somewhere waiting to be poured.

Maybe one about the painter who chides
his shoemaker for commentating on his art.

No ken, no opinions, the artist legislates.
Is that obscurely brief enough? I joke –

as if the master of a well-placed stitch
could not critique splashes of coloring.

An epistle or ode? I ask him as dinner
arrives. *I never think . . . when I write,* he snubs

my inquiry. *No one can do two things
at once and do them well.* I almost agree –

as I watch him swat flies off his salad plate
and chug another round of well-breathed wine.

I hand him my verse on water's grace, quoting him
to the evening air . . . *even fools are right sometimes.*

Requiem for the Dinner Party

Dear Friends,

After numerous attempts to be culinarily correct –
gluten-, dairy-, sugar-free, vegan, DASH, paleo,
Atkins, pescatarian, South Beach,
Mediterranean, keto –
we admit we're inept at satisfying
every palate walking through our door.
In lieu of banning in-home social time,
we request all guests abide by new rules:
bring your own food and drink.
We'll supply dishes, silver forks/spoons/knives,
glasses in every shape and size,
water filtered via Multipure,
and electric flames in the fireplace.
Avoid scents of any kind and remove your shoes
when you arrive. Select a pair of dye-free socks
made in the USA piled in baskets
native women weave to feed their families.
To keep the evening uplifting and polite,
attached please find the topics we'll avoid
and the ones we'll entertain.
When you leave, don't slam car doors.
The neighbors are noise-sensitive and we've agreed
quiet hours start when the sun slips behind the tallest evergreen.
Just so you understand, we grieve for the day invitations
simply stated date and time and RSVPs invited *yes* or *no*.

But, alas, the zeitgeist is what it is.
Acknowledge you accept the "Terms and Conditions" above.
We hope to see you Saturday promptly at six.

Disambiguation

   1. To establish a single semantic or grammatical interpretation for
   2. To remove ambiguity

Ridiculous –
this singular establishment!
Existentialists knew
life / nature / sex
could make their brown eyes blue
and poets created worlds
where the unravished bride
stands still.

Today they delight in watching
her duck and feeding her cat food
and confess – if they could find
reason or rhyme – they'd shoot
the elephant in their pjs,
watch the horse raced past the barn fall,
or wait until the chicken's ready to eat.

They'd also muster much ado
about wordy multi-values like
bear / bark / bank / deadwood /
lodestone / light / heartsease.
Life, nature, sex?
Predictable uncertainty.

And yet . . . any thinker worthy
of a thought must concede
one unputdownable truth:
even when good livers live
good lives, brown-eyed Death
 – in his deathly, deadly guise –
prides his diehard self
on ducking ambiguity.

Caged

The Minotaur goes wild
in his labyrinth,
the lawless
in scarred cinder blocks.
Vehement weeds
decimate concrete,
surging water
eons of rock.
Like rage and grief,
captive things
strain
to find a crack.
Even untamed Death
sheds
his scythe and mask
once or twice
each thousand years.
A million souls
wait on hold
while he whiffs
a moment
of pristine air.

Variations on Famous Last Words

I'm going to the bathroom to read.
Get my Swan costume ready.

And now for a final word from our sponsor –
Bring me a bulletproof vest.

Oh, you young people act like old men. You are no fun.
A party! Let's have a party.

Damn it! Don't you dare ask God to help me!
I have tried so hard to do right.

I want – I want, oh, you know what I mean, that stuff of life.
It is enough.

Don't cut the ham too thin.
My exit is the result of too many entrées.

Try to bring back the god in us to the god of the universe.
Now let me sleep.

This is the best of all possible worlds.
It will be but a momentary pang.

Oh, wow. Oh, wow. Oh, wow.
I don't think I shall get over this.

Oh, that glorious sun!
I drink the morning.

My garden . . . my garden!
It will be a pity to leave all that.

More light!
Turn up the lights. I don't want to go home in the dark.

Does nobody understand?
It is all light.

How far are we from home?
Take me home. I must go home.

This is it. I'm going, I'm going.
Tranquility.

I still live . . . poetry . . . .
Truth, truth!

I am seeing things that you know nothing of.
Hurrah, hurrah!

I am about the extent of a tenth of a gnat's eyebrow better.
This is as it should be.

It is very beautiful, but I want to go farther away.
Softly, quite softly.

Too many cigars this evening, I guess.
Gentlemen, you are all dismissed.

Oh, the beautiful Green Life again! Ah, all is well.
Give the boys a holiday.

Have I played the part well? Then applaud me as I exit.
Last words are for fools who haven't said enough.

So here it is at last, the distinguished thing!
Leave the shower curtain on the inside of the tub.

To the Book Reviewer Who Missed Too Much

You must live in a literary fog.
How could you overlook my nods to Yeats,
Williams, Ryan, Wright, Dinesen, and Bass?
Did you skip titles and epigraphs?

What's *misleading?* There's scientific proof
Neanderthals were handed a bum rap,
Seychelles frogs can hear through open mouths,
and the Milky Way burps up messy gas.

FYI: *coddiwomple* is a word.
Marx, Joyce, and Horace stated what I state
and I've chosen a dozen times to reincarnate
into this holographic universe.

Sure, I could have added notes about
Szymborska's subtle subversity,
the crime of disambiguity,
maybe a brief history of Still Lifes.

But I rely on readers – literate
and astute – not minding Googling
Abishag, Issa, *The Golden Girls*,
and the truth behind Lot's tragedy.

I'm pleased you found glee in internal rhymes –
I thought *returns/well-earned, left-behinds/sighs,*

and *white/try/reply* were audio delights –
and that you described my verbs as first-rate.

Otherwise, you misjudged the craft
it takes to write haiku, sonnets, and pantoums
next to poems with margin-to-margin lines
that re-define my previous forays.

Fair warning now: When you release your book
next fall, I'll hop on a reviewer's list.
I'll score each line with diligence and grace.
Ah, the possibilities! I can't wait.

We did all we could

– *"Point of No Return,"* MIT Scientist Predicts the Event Horizon for Earth's 6th Mass Extinction, *The Daily Galaxy*, January 6, 2018

We did all we could.
This came later –
after miscues, closed eyes,
and full-throated ignorance
singing through church pews,
school rooms,
chamber halls,
and families at supper time.

We did all we could.
This came
after sold-out masks,
cracked water lines,
the silence of bees,
roses, elephants,
children's cries,
and nature poetry.

We did all we could.
This
arrogance we'll rage
against
in our gasping grief –
that is, if we survive

later
and *extinct*.

Melt Down

Planet Earth, 2100

1. To whom it may concern:

According to the High Command,
the projector crashed last night.
Lasers burned. All freestanding 3-Ds
are lying on the ground,
two-dimensionally.
Someone got something wrong.

Everything – the zillion holograms
from the biggest bang to a turning maple leaf,
from titanosaurs to fairyflies,
from DaVinci, Newton, Einstein
to geniuses almost-born – collapsed.

Command believes, despite
earth's restless beauty and its lurking cruelty,
humans might have handled virtuals
like marriage, stillbirths, work,
vaccines, genocides, religions,
and governments of every sort.
They regret the end point came too soon.

We Mid-levelers on the ground
won't forget how Humankind amused

with little lives that stumbled through.
Here and there, one got it right.
It's not their fault plans to reboot are shelved.

Crews are sweeping up their left-behinds,
erasing all biped stains.
The latest update on the new 4-D:
It's in its final testing stage.
Expect progress reports next week.

2. From those it concerns:

We don't know why the lights went out.
Grounded nose to stone,
we're bristled into random piles
like used confetti or stained paper plates.

We don't know why the lights went out.
We were going about our goings-on –
bemoaning fires / earthquakes / hurricanes,
walking the dog, untying toddlers' shoes,
check-listing a day that rolled out as it should –
when we splattered on the ground.

We don't know why. The lights went out
and we reduced to an ant-eye view.
If only we could raise our heads
above the grass. Do we still have brains?
We're thinking, so that indicates.

We don't know. Why the lights went out
for unscheduled maintenance is a mystery.
When officials arrive to pump us up,
we'll ask them to explain.
It's not inconceivable
we'll believe anything they say.

Saving

*Are the people who live inside [Manú National Park]
good for it or bad? And is the park good for them?*
– Emma Marris, "Peru's World Apart," *National Geographic,* June
2016

Dimes drop into the cardboard box on Sister's desk.
For missionaries, she says, who preach Good News
to people who need to be saved. From what
or for? A child, you don't ask. Count coins.
Wonder how much saving costs.

*

The photograph: wild girl – full lips,
barely fierce brown eyes, a black avalanche of hair –
floating on a river in Manú. A tamarin crowns her head.
A pet, the caption says, and she, a Matsigenka child.
Eleven-syllables in her name.

*

The park: saved from rubber barons,
loggers, miners, and extractors of natural gas.
Monkeys: saved from tribes that arrow-hunt.
No guns allowed. Monkeys move fast.
The forest: saved by seeds saved monkeys drop.

*

Tonight you'll recycle the magazine and stack up
prayers for people who have no time for news,

good or not; who live in tree pole shacks,
in cardboard boxes under every overpass,
in piles of rags squirming in doorways.

⋆

You don't know whom you're praying to or what
you're praying for. Is praying the right word?
Like saving, it mystifies. Ponder the sky
that drapes over the Manú. Wonder out loud
to anyone who'll hear, *Does saving ever stop?*

Should You Ever Start to Pray –

and you know who you are –
avoid bedsides, pews, steepled
fingertips, and words mumbled
through a billion mouths.
Forget pleading with angels, saints,
gods, or the aunt who died last year.
They don't want bothering
about lost jobs or driving grief
when they're tending broken wings
and holding tides in place.
Rather, from your yard – front or back –
launch crucial questions
toward the random Universe:
Where was Light before Chaos arrived?
What's the space between despair and hope?
How many lies can one mind tolerate?
The truth – if you care to know:
curiosity is blessing in disguise.
Questions are enough.
Of course, answers may slip
through a wobbly black hole
like mists of poetry rising
from fallow fields, like hums
of rogue planets soothing
failing stars.

A Case for Choosing Sudden Death

And for the finale of your next life,
will you rely again on happenstance
or fate? Or would you consider setting up
your own how/when/where/why and test
the luxury of pre-planned suddenness?

Think about etching your name
on bullets sprayed across a parking lot
or arriving on time for a lightning strike,
mudslide, earthquake, plane crash,
or dam-break easing you downstream.

How about a clog or clot that takes you
out moments after EMTs arrive?
You'd be a lesson – fitting and precise –
for the new trainee who's yet to feel
the feel of someone's final breath.

Or persuade the novelist you stabbed
two lives ago to meet you at Third and Oak.
His car will jump a solid red
just as you cross between the lines.
You'll revel in the irony.

By now you've learned there's no right way
to die – you've varied the event
a dozen times – so a pre-arrangement

might intrigue. Rather than months
propped up in bed – body-bound,

soul nipping at clouds – you'll ascend
without worries of what you've left
behind or who's waiting ahead.
And consider this: if your penciling out
is accurate enough, the last lines

of the last poem you write will celebrate
the brilliance of your choice, perhaps
prophesy your next return after,
of course, well-earned breathing time
and space stretched out among the stars.

Epilogue

Before scratches on cave walls
        and raspy voices learned
                to moan, groan, grunt, and growl.

Before fires took and gave
        and crops settled tribes in place
                and prophets shouted to the deaf.

Before black holes, meteors,
        and asteroids wearied of themselves
                and planet-killing stars got caught.

Before Chaos ordered elements
        and the elegance of Time
                joined *before* to *beyond.*

Before the Infinite loped across
        unkempt galaxies imagining
                orchids, butterflies, and bird-filled trees.

Before Creation assured deep Voids
        that *Let there be* relieves the dark,
                a Voice whispered from somewhere –

an echo of a long-forgotten thought? –
        As soon as Life sips Its first breath,
                does It suspect It's conceived to die?

Acknowledgments

Grateful acknowledgment is made to the editors of the publications who first printed these poems, sometimes as a different version.

Abstract Magazine: Contemporary Expressions, "33 Sententious Epigraphs That May – or Not – Prompt a Poem," "Marx Was Right," "Stirring"

Amethyst Review, "Epilogue" published as "Before the Beginning," "*Since feeling comes first*," "To each her saint"

Cross Review, "Phonaesthetics"

Gyroscope Review, "Evidence," "Re-Entry Interview," "Twenty-Five Years After Sodom and Gomorrah: Lot's Older Daughter Makes Her Case," "What's in a Name?"

Haiku Journal, from "Haiku: Perennial Wisdom": "on a winter night"

Ink Sweat and Tears, from "Haiku: Perennial Wisdom": "a hummingbird dines," "crisped leaves," "early spring chill," "morning alert"

Kosmos Quarterly, "Should You Ever Start to Pray –"

Mezzo Cammin, "For Bob, an Express Parking Lot Bus Driver on the Early Morning Shift at Portland International," "Triolet"

Open: Journal of Arts & Letters, "An Amateur Photographer Reads Szymborska's 'No Title Required'," "Thoughts on a Translation"

Panoplyzine, "What I Know of 'Good'," "In the Women's Locker Room"

Peacock Journal, "A Novice's Confession," "*For God sake hold your tongue and let me love*"

Star 82 Review, "History"

These Fragile Lilacs, "A Few Words About Inspiration"

The Manhattanville Review, "Variations on Famous Last Words"

The New Verse News, "Here, a Holding On," "We did all we could"

The Opiate, "10 Variations on the 50 Most Quoted Lines of Poetry"

The Poeming Pigeon, "Attention: Costco General Manager/Re: Why I Returned My Dead Christmas Tree on January 5," "Everything Good Between Us"

Thirteen Ways, "What's Wrong With This Picture?"

Verseweavers, "Sonnet for a 25th Wedding Anniversary"

VoiceCatcher: a journal of women's voices & visions, "Reading *Bailing the River* While Waiting for the Ruby-Throated Hummingbird to Dine on Crocosmia"

Word Fountain, "Hiking, Formerly Known as Hill Walking," "To the Police Officer Who Let Me Off the Hook"

Zingara Poetry Review, "Overheard"

About the Author

From associate professor of English to management trainer to retiree, Carolyn Martin has journeyed from New Jersey through California to Oregon to discover Douglas firs, months of rain, and dry summers. She believes that poetry is the way her mind interacts with the world – in images, rhythms, sounds, and intensities of language. After years of writing academic papers and business books, she's settled into the joyful challenge of translating experience into as few words as possible. Her aesthetic is embodied in Jack Kerouac's comment in *Dharma Bums*: *One day I will find the right words, and they will be simple*; and in Galway Kinnell's statement, *To me, poetry is somebody standing up ... and saying, with as little concealment as possible, what it is for him or her to be on earth at this moment.* Her poems attempt to be simple in words as they grapple with the complexity of living on earth today.

Carolyn's poems and book reviews have appeared in publications throughout North America and the UK, and her third collection, *Thin Places*, was released by Kelsay Books in 2017. She is currently the poetry editor of *Kosmos Quarterly, journal for global transformation*.

Find Carolyn at www.carolynmartinpoet.com.

About the Press

Unsolicited Press was founded in 2012. The team seeks to publish fantastic and intelligent poetry, fiction, and creative nonfiction. Learn more at www.unsolicitedpress.com.

www.ingramcontent.com/pod-product-compliance
Lightning Source LLC
Chambersburg PA
CBHW020123130526
44591CB00032B/462